PROTEIN
SHAKES
FOR THE
BRAIN

PROTEIN SHAKES

SHAKES

FOR THE

BRAIN

Michel Noir, Ph.D. & Bernard Croisile, M.D., Ph.D.

Middle School of Plainville LIC
Plainville, CT

New York Chicago San Francisco Lisbon London Madrid Mexico City
Milan New Delhi San Juan Seoul Singapore Sydney Toronto

The **McGraw·Hill** Companies

Library of Congress Cataloging-in-Publication Data

Noir, Michel, 1944–
    Protein shakes for the brain : 90 games and exercises to work your mind's muscle to the max
/ Michel Noir and Bernard Croisile. — 1st ed.
       p.   cm.
    Includes index.
    ISBN 978-0-07-162836-5 (alk. paper)
    1. Logic puzzles.   2. Word games.   3. Intellect—Problems, exercises, etc.   4. Brain.
I. Croisile, Bernard.   II. Title.

GV1493.N65   2009
793.73—dc22   2009000963

1 2 3 4 5 6 7 8 9 10 11 12 13 14 15 16 17 18 19 20 21 22 CTP/CTP 0 9

ISBN 978-0-07-162836-5
MHID   0-07-162836-3

McGraw-Hill books are available at special quantity discounts to use as premiums and sales
promotions or for use in corporate training programs. To contact a representative, please visit the
Contact Us pages at www.mhprofessional.com.

This book is printed on acid-free paper.

Contents

Why Does My Brain Need a Protein Shake? vii

JUST STARTING OUT
Easy Exercises 1

GETTING FIT
Medium Exercises. 39

IRON MAN
Hard Exercises 77

Solutions 117

Why Does My Brain Need a Protein Shake?

Increasingly, scientific evidence tells us that our minds don't *have* to deteriorate as we age—there are things we can do now to dramatically increase the probability of staying mentally and physically fit throughout our lives. This is good news indeed, because mental fitness and agility are so directly connected to a good quality of life. Physical exercise, good nutrition, social connection with others, and mental stimulation all play important parts in ensuring that our brains remain sharp and agile.

Over the past 25 years, scientists and physicians affiliated with medical schools and universities all over the world have followed and tested large groups of people to try to understand why some people stay mentally sharp over the span of their lives and other people don't. As a result, we now have a significant body of scientific research in an area called "cognitive reserve." Cognitive reserve involves the brain's ability to create new neural pathways and connections that can be used as a mental savings account, a reserve to be drawn upon in times of need. The research supports the hypothesis that many people continue to operate at a high mental level throughout their lives by building these brain reserves.

Several studies support the hypothesis of cognitive reserve and reinforce the importance of good physical health in keeping the brain fit. One such study is the famous Nun's Study described in *Aging with Grace*, in which Dr. David Snowdon, a neurologist, and his colleagues followed 700 nuns over more than 20 years. Two extremely important findings have come out of this study: first, there is a link between vascular episodes, such as stroke and heart attack, and Alzheimer's and dementia; and second, stimulating intellectual activity can provide protection from many types of cognitive decline.

Other ongoing studies have come to similar conclusions. The Bronx Aging Study, led by neurologist Dr. Joe Verghese and published in *The New England Journal of Medicine*, has followed almost 500 people for more than 20 years, observing what they actually do in their lives and what the relationship is between these choices and brain health. The research has found that people who participated in mentally stimulating activities, such as interactive games and dancing, four times a week had a 65 to 75 percent better probability of remaining sharp than those who did not participate in these activities.

Dr. David Bennett at Rush University Medical Center has recently come to the same conclusion after following more than 2,000 people for years. Over time, 134 people died. None of them had been diagnosed with Alzheimer's or even mild cognitive decline. But 36 percent of them had the severe tangles and plaques of Alzheimer's. This positive news reinforces the "use it or lose it" philosophy; these people had built up enough brain reserves to show no clinical signs of disease, meaning they still exhibited good thinking skills.

We encourage you to challenge yourself to learn at every opportunity by learning a new language or a new musical instrument or new and more complex tunes with an old one, reading, dancing, or taking a class. These are all effective tools to keep your mind sharp. But sometimes your brain needs a quick shot in the arm, a quick burst of energy—that's why we developed *Protein Shakes for the Brain*. Doing the puzzles in this book is a quick and easy way to give your mind's muscle a little boost and keep those neural pathways growing.

JUST STARTING OUT

Easy Exercises

Warm-Ups

Do you know the answers to these common-knowledge questions? Shake up your brain and find out.

1. Who wrote the short-story "The Fall of the House of Usher"?
   a. Emily Brontë   **b.** D. H. Lawrence   **c.** Edgar Allan Poe

2. Which type of ship did Christopher Columbus use to sail to America?
   a. schooner   **b.** caravel   **c.** trimaran

3. Which sport is Kobe Bryant famous for?
   a. swimming   **b.** karate   **c.** basketball

4. Which one of these snakes is not deadly for humans?
   a. viper   **b.** cobra   **c.** rat snake

5. Which country does tiramisu, a delicious chocolate and coffee cake, come from?
   a. Italy   **b.** Spain   **c.** Romania

6. What was the name of Sherlock Holmes's famous friend?
   a. James   **b.** William   **c.** Watson

7. What color do you get when you mix yellow and blue together?
   a. purple   **b.** red   **c.** green

8. What is celebrated in the United States on July 4th?
   a. The approval of the Declaration of Independence
   b. The signing of the Declaration of Independence
   c. The first battle in the Revolutionary War

Warm-Ups

Do you know the answers to these common-knowledge questions? Shake up your brain and find out.

1. Which one of these is *not* an insect?

   a. spider   **b.** flea   **c.** butterfly

2. Who created the beloved Simpsons cartoon family?

   a. Matt Groening **b.** Bob Kane **c.** Stan Lee

3. Which one of these characters did Walt Disney *not* create?

   a. Donald Duck **b.** Pluto **c.** Popeye the Sailor

4. During which century did Mozart live?

   a. 17th   **b.** 18th   **c.** 19th

5. Which famous battle did General Custer die at?

   a. Bull Run **b.** Little Bighorn **c.** Waterloo

6. Which country originated the sauna?

   a. Finland **b.** Norway **c.** Sweden

7. Which animal is considered man's best friend?

   a. cat   **b.** cow   **c.** dog

8. Who directed the movie *Jurassic Park*?

   a. Martin Scorsese **b.** Steven Spielberg **c.** Robert Altman

Daily Workout

Can you remember in which year these historical events occurred?

1. The first man on the moon

   _____

2. The sinking of the Titanic

   _____

3. The Boston Tea Party

   _____

4. The Wall Street crash

   _____

5. The discovery of America by Christopher Columbus

   _____

6. The end of the Vietnam War

   _____

7. The fall of the Berlin Wall

   _____

8. The Declaration of Independence

   _____

Daily Workout

Can you remember in which year these historical events occurred?

1. The start of World War II

_____

2. The battle of the Little Bighorn

_____

3. The Chernobyl disaster

_____

4. The death of Princess Diana

_____

5. The Los Angeles Olympic Games

_____

6. The start of Ronald Reagan's presidency

_____

7. The crowning of Queen Elizabeth II of the United Kingdom

_____

8. The death of William Shakespeare

_____

Interval Training

Can you put back together the 20 words that have been split into two syllables and spread across the grid? Watch out, each syllable can be used only once!

TIP: *All words belong to the category "Fruits and Vegetables."*

fruit	ly	sweet	beet	nach
pi	pars	ca	bread	go
me	dur	chee	ki	per
pars	kin	on	lon	rrot
man	wi	root	le	quat
ion	barb	mon	ley	tuce
ckle	kum	pump	corn	pep
rhu	nip	let	ban	spi

Your answers:

1. _____
2. _____
3. _____
4. _____
5. _____
6. _____
7. _____
8. _____
9. _____
10. _____

11. _____
12. _____
13. _____
14. _____
15. _____
16. _____
17. _____
18. _____
19. _____
20. _____

Interval Training

Can you put back together the 20 words that have been split into two syllables and spread across the grid? Watch out, each syllable can be used only once!

TIP: *All words belong to the category "Capital Cities."*

Lon	A	Li	lin	rich
ney	Ma	ran	Pa	blin
lo	Bei	Zu	ro	thens
War	Os	lin	jing	saw
don	Ber	Nas	noi	Teh
drid	to	Syd	ma	rain
Tal	Bah	Mos	sau	Cai
cow	Ha	Qui	Du	ris

Your answers:

1. _____   11. _____

2. _____   12. _____

3. _____   13. _____

4. _____   14. _____

5. _____   15. _____

6. _____   16. _____

7. _____   17. _____

8. _____   18. _____

9. _____   19. _____

10. _____   20. _____

Lateral Rows

For each row, circle which of the three words is spelled correctly.

1. insolvancy   insolvency   insulvency
2. valuable   valewable   valluable
3. accordance   acordance   accordence
4. occurrence   ocurrence   occurrance
5. insaucing   insourcing   insourssing
6. literature   litterature   literiture
7. oceanollogy   oceanology   oshenology
8. manigement   managemant   management
9. yogourt   yoggurt   yogurt
10. trainee   trainy   trainnee
11. occupency   occupancy   occupenssy
12. hazard   hayzard   hazad
13. occlusive   oclusive   occlussive
14. intergrate   integreat   integrate
15. yungster   youngster   youngsta
16. azure   azzure   azurre

Lateral Rows

For each row, circle which of the three words is spelled correctly.

1. vitamin   vittamin   vitammin
2. babywhere   babywear   babiwear
3. dabbler   debbler   dabler
4. tobaco   tobbaco   tobacco
5. weakend   weekend   weekkend
6. welth   wealth   wellth
7. fruitful   frootful   fruitfull
8. jockee   jocky   jockey
9. abilitty   abillity   ability
10. beach   bich   beatch
11. ozon   ozone   osone
12. hiccup   hickup   hicup
13. geneealogy   geneallogy   genealogy
14. varsitty   varsity   varsety
15. junior   joonior   junier
16. docter   doctor   docktor

Bio-Feedback

Whose life is described below?

I was born on July 6, 1907, in my parents' house "La Casa Azul" in Coyoacán, Mexico. My father, who died in 1941, was born in Pforzheim, Germany, and was the son of a painter and goldsmith. Even though my parents' marriage was rather unhappy, they still had four daughters. I am the third.

In 1913, I was affected by poliomyelitis and my right leg became thinner than the left one. I always wore long skirts to hide this.

I suffered serious injuries and fractures in a bus accident on September 17, 1925, and had to undergo 35 operations. Following the accident I turned to painting, which helped me enormously during my recovery. My paintings are full of color and greatly influenced by the indigenous Mexican culture. Monkeys, a symbol of Mexican mythology, often recur, as well as Christian and Jewish themes, and I liked to combine tradition and surrealism. My self-portraits, in particular, were a major part of my work.

In 1929, I married the famous Mexican painter Diego Rivera, whose work I had always admired. Our marriage was stormy, and we both had extramarital relationships, one of mine being with Leon Trotsky.

In 1939, I was invited to France by André Breton and given the opportunity to do an exhibition. As the first painting by a 20th-century Mexican artist ever purchased by the internationally renowned Louvre, "The Frame," one of my seminal works, was displayed at the exhibition.

I died from pulmonary embolism on July 13, 1954.

Bio-Feedback

Whose life is described below?

I was born on March 2, 1931, in Privolnoye, Russia, and faced a tough childhood under Stalin's regime. I lived through World War II, and my experience during the German occupation of Russia between August 1942 and February 1943 had a great impact on my perception of life and my professional career.

In September 1950, I started studying law at Moscow University and later joined the Communist Party of the Soviet Union (CPSU) as a candidate member. I also met my future wife, Raisa, in Moscow. We married in 1953 and moved back to my home region after my graduation in 1955.

I was made a member of the CPSU in 1971 and moved on to the politburo in 1979, with full membership in 1980. My positions gave me many traveling opportunities, and it was on one such trip that I met the British Prime Minister Margaret Thatcher in 1984. On March 11, 1985, I was elected General Secretary of the Communist Party. I was the first party leader born after the revolution and I tried to reform the party. In 1988, I announced the decision to abandon the Brezhnev Doctrine and to allow the countries of the Eastern bloc to develop freely.

In March and April 1989, I was elected Chairman of the Supreme Soviet and thus head of state during the very first free election since 1917 in the Soviet Union. I had close relationships with leaders like President Ronald Reagan and Margaret Thatcher. I was awarded the Otto Hahn Peace Medal in Gold that same year and the Nobel Peace Prize on October 15, 1990.

On March 15, 1990, I was elected the first and the only President of the Soviet Union by the Congress of People's Deputies. After a great crisis, I agreed to dissolve the Soviet Union on December 17, 1991, and I resigned from my position on December 25. I am the most famous person with *naevus flammeus*, a crimson birthmark on top of my head.

The Proper Form

Pay attention to the shape and position of the six icons in the grid. Then turn the page and continue the exercise.

The Proper Form

Can you place all six elements correctly back into the grid?

TIP: *The fields where an item is supposed to be are colored in blue!*

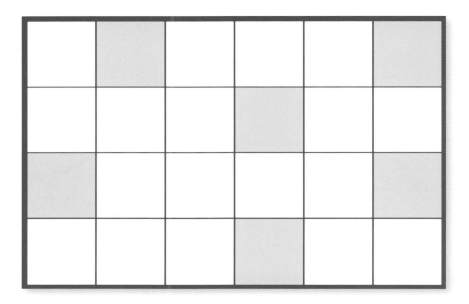

The Proper Form

Pay attention to the shape and position of the six icons in the grid. Then turn the page and continue the exercise.

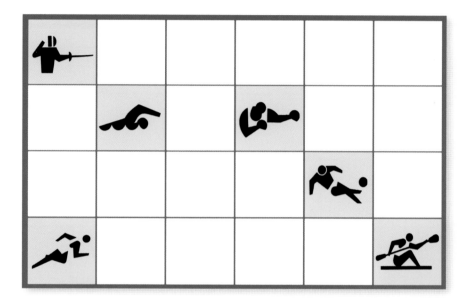

The Proper Form

Can you place all six elements correctly back into the grid?

TIP: The fields where an item is supposed to be are colored in blue!

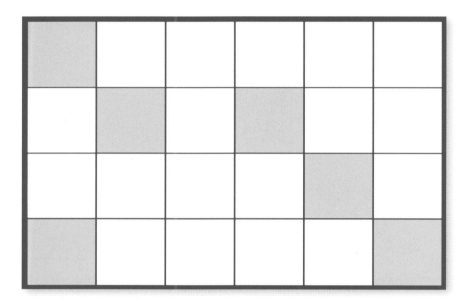

No Pain, No _____

Complete the following idioms with the missing word.

1. Elephant in the _____

2. A lick and a _____

3. Icing on the _____

4. Larger than _____

5. Ugly _____

6. Learn the _____

7. Vicious _____

8. Jump through _____

9. Cool as a _____

10. Just off the _____

11. Basket _____

12. Deliver the _____

13. U- _____

14. Eat my _____

15. Get away with _____

No Pain, No _____

Complete the following popular dishes with the missing word.

1. Fortune _____
2. Chili con _____
3. Roast _____
4. Moon _____
5. Chocolate chip _____
6. Hush _____
7. Shrimp _____
8. Hot fudge _____
9. Onion _____
10. Peanut _____
11. Devil's food _____
12. Mashed _____
13. Corn on the _____
14. Macaroni and _____
15. Layer _____

Working the Memory Muscle

Take a minute to memorize the six words below without looking at the bottom half of the page.

shrimp

cow

cupboard

design

elephant

part

Now cover up the list of words and answer the following questions:

1. What, if any, animals are on the list?

_____

2. Name the abstract words on the list.

_____

3. Which word is the shortest on the list?

_____

Working the Memory Muscle

Take a minute to memorize the six words below without looking at the bottom half of the page.

tea

document

feather

happiness

chef

certainty

Now cover up the list of words and answer the following questions:

1. Which drink is on the list?

_____

2. What, if any, profession is on the list?

_____

3. Which word from the list can be found on a bird?

_____

The Final Rep

Carefully read the following four sentences and memorize the last word of each one. Then turn the page and continue.

Each summer, Luke used to go salmon fishing with his cousin.

Mary's mother always used to serve her roast lamb with sweet potatoes.

Francis and Chloe painted their living room the year they moved into their new house.

Mark finally called the plumber after the toilet had been leaking for three days.

The Final Rep

According to what you have just read, can you answer this question?

A. Which dish did Mary's mother serve with the sweet potatoes?

- Fried chicken
- Grilled sausages
- Roast lamb

B. Can you write down the last word of each sentence?

Sentence 1: _____

Sentence 2: _____

Sentence 3: _____

Sentence 4: _____

The Final Rep

Carefully read the following four sentences and memorize the last word of each one. Then turn the page and continue.

After the thunderstorm, the leaves of the chestnut trees were strewn across the park lawn.

When I arrived, the concierge was sweeping the front yard.

Yesterday, five reckless mountain climbers triggered an avalanche close to the resort.

Janis had her camera stolen while she was visiting the old city.

The Final Rep

According to what you have just read, can you answer this question?

A. Because of what could chestnut leaves be found all over the park?

- Tornado
- Thunderstorm
- Rain

B. Can you write down the last word of each sentence?

Sentence 1: _____

Sentence 2: _____

Sentence 3: _____

Sentence 4: _____

Opposing Muscle Groups

A. Find the opposite words for the 10 following words. The first letter has been given as a clue.

1. Slim: f_____

6. high: l_____

2. ugly: b_____

7. true: f_____

3. nice: m_____

8. wet: d_____

4. dirty: c_____

9. cautious: c_____

5. strong: w_____

10. wide: n_____

B. Which are the two synonyms in each word series?

1. mom   woman   relative   mother   ancestor

2. entry   exit   door   gate   threshold

3. issue   catastrophe   delay   cancellation   problem

4. tendency   look   reflection   appearance   character

5. diarrhea   constipation   nausea   digestion   queasiness

Opposing Muscle Groups

A. Find the opposite words for the 10 following words. The first letter has been given as a clue.

1. honest: d_____   **6.** thick: t_____

2. big: s_____   **7.** closed: o_____

3. soft: h_____   **8.** frequent: s_____

4. courageous: c_____   **9.** young: o_____

5. good: b_____   **10.** junior: s_____

B. Which are the two synonyms in each word series?

1. excellent   great   flawless   fantastic   perfect

2. sadness   resentment   disgust   grief   fear

3. omen   magic   astrology   witchcraft   jinx

4. pitcher   bottle   flagon   recipient   decanter

5. alphabet   missive   writing   letter   parcel

Muscle Groups

Sort all the words in the list below into four categories and then give each category a title.

bologna	sponge	brie	cheddar	liverwurst
cupcake	gorgonzola	gouda	ham	hot dog
pound	leg of lamb	mozzarella	fruit	prosciutto
roast beef	salami	spare ribs	steak	tiramisu

TITLE	TITLE	TITLE	TITLE
_____	_____	_____	_____
_____	_____	_____	_____
_____	_____	_____	_____
_____	_____	_____	_____

Muscle Groups

Sort all the words in the list below into four categories and then give each category a title.

acacia	apricot	blueberry	cherry	chicory
corn	date	endive	escarole	geranium
laurel	lettuce	moss	nettle	oat
pineapple	rice	rocket	rye	wheat

TITLE	TITLE	TITLE	TITLE

The Incomplete Workout

Look at the picture below. One tile is missing. Select the missing piece.

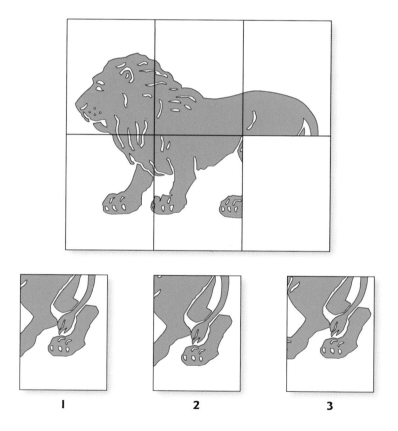

1   2   3

The Incomplete Workout

Look at the picture below. One tile is missing. Select the missing piece.

1   2   3

The Answers Are in the Stars

Of the nine words in each list below, only six can be placed in the star. Arrows indicate the direction in which each word is placed. To assist you, one letter has already been placed in each star. Try to fill in the two stars in five minutes or less.

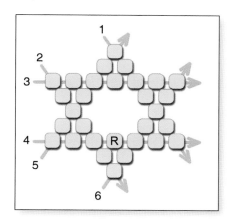

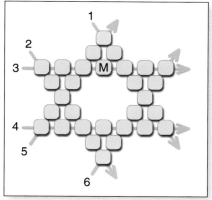

DIPLOMA	CHARITY
DRIZZLE	COMMUNE
ECLIPSE	CONCEPT
EPISODE	GRANITE
EXAMPLE	MEANING
FURRIER	METHANE
PAPRIKA	PLASTIC
POLLARD	PRIMARY
SKIMMER	SAXHORN

The Answers Are in the Stars

Of the nine words in each list below, only six can be placed in the star. Arrows indicate the direction in which each word is placed. To assist you, one letter has already been placed in each star. Try to fill in the two stars in five minutes or less.

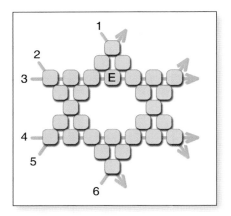
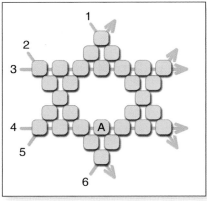

APPAREL	PACKAGE
AVIDITY	PANACHE
CAPTION	PARSECS
CURETTE	PARSNIP
LANDING	PREFACE
LOTTERY	PREMISE
NAIVETE	PAJAMAS
RENEGER	SAWMILL
WOODCUT	SOILAGE

Muscle Memory

Carefully look at the following composition. Then turn the page and continue the exercise.

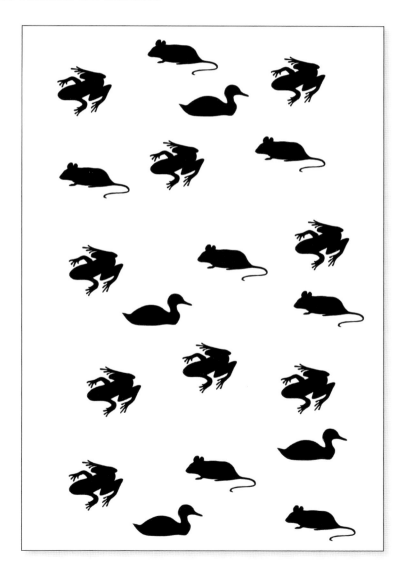

Muscle Memory

Can you answer the following questions?

1. How many frogs did you see?

_____

2. To which side do the rats turn their heads?

_____

3. What is the third animal in the composition?

_____

Muscle Memory

Carefully look at the following composition. Then turn the page and continue the exercise.

Muscle Memory

Can you answer the following questions?

1. How many objects are in the picture?

   _____

2. To which side of the glass are the straws turned?

   _____

3. How many salt shakers are there?

   _____

Pencils Up!

Link the eight blue flowers on this page without raising your pencil. You cannot touch the other flowers, and you cannot go between two flowers more than once!

Pencils Up!

Link the 10 red maple leaves on this page without raising your pencil. You cannot touch the other leaves, and you cannot go between two leaves more than once!

Medium Exercises

Warm-Ups

Do you know the answers to these common-knowledge questions? Shake up your brain and find out.

1. Which planet is the largest of the solar system?
   a. Saturn   **b.** Jupiter   **c.** Uranus

2. How many pictures per seconds are there in today's cartoons?
   a. 1   **b.** 18.   **c.** 24

3. Which day is the Irish St. Patrick's Day celebrated on?
   a. March 12   **b.** March 17   **c.** March 22

4. What symbol is used for the chemical element copper?
   a. Cu   **b.** C   **c.** Co

5. Who wrote *The Adventures of Huckleberry Finn*?
   a. Thomas Hardy   **b.** Henry James   **c.** Mark Twain

6. Which animal lays eggs and has a duck's beak, a beaver's tail, and an otter's legs?
   a. civet   **b.** platypus   **c.** badger

7. Which of these countries is not included in the E.U.?
   a. Italy   **b.** Bulgaria   **c.** Switzerland

8. Which English harbor did the *Titanic* leave from?
   a. Liverpool   **b.** Newcastle   **c.** Southampton

Warm-Ups

Do you know the answers to these common-knowledge questions? Shake up your brain and find out.

1. In which Indian city is the Taj Mahal?
   a. Delhi   **b.** Varanasi   **c.** Agra

2. What is Popeye the Sailor's sweetheart called?
   a. Rose Pearl   **b.** Olive Oyl   **c.** Betty Boop

3. Which currency is used in Morocco?
   a. Ruble   **b.** Lira   **c.** Dirham

4. How many Oscars was the legendary movie *Titanic* awarded?
   a. 9   **b.** 10   **c.** 11

5. In Roman mythology, Mars was the god of what?
   a. War   **b.** Love   **c.** Wine

6. What is the largest state in North America?
   a. Arizona   **b.** Texas   **c.** Alaska

7. Which famous singer is the Japanese artist and musician Yoko Ono associated with?
   a. John Lennon   **b.** David Bowie   **c.** Sting

8. What is the name of the highest national honor in newspaper journalism, literary achievement, and musical composition in the United States?
   a. Academy Awards **b.** Pulitzer Prize   **c.** Bancroft Prize

Daily Workout

Can you remember in which year these historical events occurred?

1. The collapse of the Soviet Union

_____

2. The Yalta Conference

_____

3. The Battle of Waterloo

_____

4. The atomic bombing of Hiroshima

_____

5. The beginning of the presidency of Ronald Reagan

_____

6. The abolition of slavery in the United States

_____

7. The death of actress Audrey Hepburn

_____

8. The start of the construction of the Brooklyn Bridge

_____

Daily Workout

Can you remember in which year these historical events occurred?

1. The invention of the cinematograph

_____

2. The dedication of the Statue of Liberty

_____

3. The construction of the Eiffel Tower

_____

4. The beginning of the American Civil War

_____

5. The launch of Sputnik 1

_____

6. The start of the French revolution

_____

7. The Great Fire of New York

_____

8. The death of Julius Caesar

_____

Interval Training

Can you put back together the 20 multisyllabic words that have been split and spread across the grid? Watch out, each syllable can be used only once, and the splits may not necessarily be the syllable splits you find in the dictionary!

TIP: *All words belong to the category "Trees."*

ba	li	ju	ce	quo	a
sy	ca	ssa	ni	lin	se
no	nut	pa	but	bab	wil
ce	red	o	ia	mo	fras
tree	lia	ma	dar	lock	mag
ca	horn	tal	beam	lip	hem
low	gus	dar	fir	mi	trum
glas	den	dou	per	tu	ple
ca	cia	sa	more	sa	ter

Your answers:

1. _____

2. _____

3. _____

4. _____

5. _____

6. _____

7. _____

8. _____

9. _____

10. _____

11. _____

12. _____

13. _____

14. _____

15. _____

16. _____

17. _____

18. _____

19. _____

20. _____

Interval Training

Can you put back together the 20 multisyllabic words that have been split and spread across the grid? Watch out, each syllable can be used only once, and the splits may not necessarily be the syllable splits you find in the dictionary!

TIP: *All words belong to the category "Home, Furniture, and Living."*

fur	pho	cham	top	cre	to
ca	ton	re	sol	cli	ner
pain	ter	fu	se	fa	role
cas	graph	ni	net	den	ches
li	bi	shing	side	bed	coun
ting	ter	can	ter	za	room
ving	ment	wa	cup	ding	board
board	ber	pa	a	so	ra
screen	dle	field	fol	pot	part

Your answers:

1. _____   11. _____

2. _____   12. _____

3. _____   13. _____

4. _____   14. _____

5. _____   15. _____

6. _____   16. _____

7. _____   17. _____

8. _____   18. _____

9. _____   19. _____

10. _____   20. _____

Lateral Rows

For each row, circle which of the three words is spelled correctly.

1. kosher   kosha   cosher

2. dossent   docent   docant

3. mooze   moozze   moose

4. numb   num   numm

5. heddonism   hedonism   hedonnism

6. claster   clustor   cluster

7. macaber   macabor   macabre

8. bizarre   bizzare   bizare

9. brue   broo   brew

10. humble   humbble   humbel

11. backbored   backboard   backbord

12. verticol   vertical   verticul

13. goblet   goblit   gobblet

14. amayzing   amasing   amazing

15. gobbsmacked   gobsmecked   gobsmacked

16. thiara   tiara   tyara

Lateral Rows

For each row, circle which of the three words is spelled correctly.

1. bobslay — bobsleigh — bobsley
2. docility — docilitty — docillity
3. bibblical — biblical — bibliccal
4. amused — amuzed — amoosed
5. musli — muesly — muesli
6. nugget — nuggit — nuget
7. cloo — klue — clue
8. maccaroni — macaroni — macarroni
9. thyme — thime — thymme
10. wuful — woeful — woful
11. onwards — onwerds — onwarts
12. mucos — muckus — mucous
13. boilled — boyled — boiled
14. mudgard — mudguard — madguard
15. jubillee — jubilee — jubily
16. kernell — kernnel — kernel

Bio-Feedback

Whose life is described below?

I was born in London on April 29, 1957. My father, who was Irish and who never showed much interest in me or my older sister, died when I was just 15. My mother, sister, and I lived in a working class area, where I was often bullied for my "posh" accent and for being Jewish. I quickly learned to master the local accent in order to fit in. Sometimes I think this was the start of my acting career.

I tended to get into trouble during my teen years, with shoplifting and other petty crimes appearing on my record. To keep me from turning to a life of crime, I was sent to a boarding school, which I hated but which was where I first discovered my greatest interests in life: woodworking and acting. I made my first appearance on the screen at the age of 14 in the film *Sunday Bloody Sunday*. I left that school after two years and transferred to a different one, after which I calmed down considerably and stopped acting out.

At this school, I decided to become a cabinetmaker but was not accepted for my apprenticeship. Instead I was accepted at the British Vic Theatre School and graduated after three years. The film *My Beautiful Laundrette* and *A Room with a View* are my most well-known performances, and I have won two Academy Awards for Best Actor for my performances as Daniel Plainview in 2007 and Christy Brown in 1989.

Bio-Feedback

Whose life is described below?

I was born in Manchester, England, on May 22, 1959, to an Irish Catholic immigrant family. My father was a hospital porter and my mother was a librarian. When I was young, while other kids my age were listening to pop, I became obsessed with 1960s girl groups, Marianne Faithful, Timi Yuro, and Sandie Shaw and was also fascinated by the soap opera "Coronation Street," James Dean, and Oscar Wilde.

After passing three O-levels at Stretford Technical School, I briefly worked at the Inland Revenue, collecting taxes, and then decided to leave and concentrate on my music. In 1978, I briefly played in a punk band called the Nosebleeds. After a few concerts we were reviewed in the major music magazine *NME*. The Nosebleeds soon split, and I followed one of the members, Billy Duffy, into the band Slaughter & the Dogs. After a major failed audition, I left the band. I spent a while writing on popular culture and published two books, including *James Dean Is Not Dead*.

In 1982, I formed the band I became so famous for with the guitarist Johnny Marr. We became a huge success in the U.K., Australia, and Ireland and were considered cult favorites in the United States. Our band split in 1987 after our guitarist and I fell out, and I went on to pursue a successful solo career.

The Proper Form

Pay attention to the shape and position of the eight icons in the grid. Then turn the page and continue the exercise.

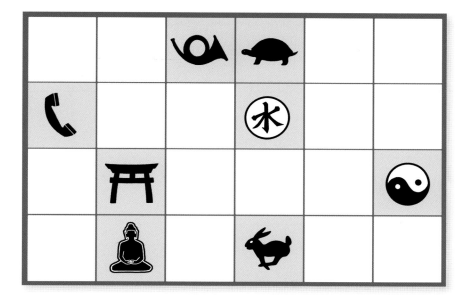

The Proper Form

Can you place all eight elements correctly back into the grid?

TIP: *The fields where an item is supposed to be are colored in blue!*

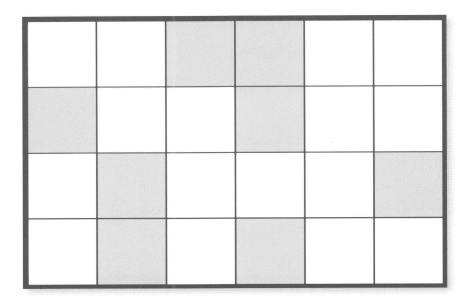

The Proper Form

Pay attention to the shape and position of the eight icons in the grid. Then turn the page and continue the exercise.

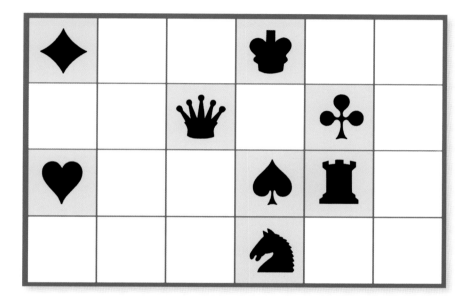

The Proper Form

Can you place all eight elements correctly back into the grid?

TIP: The fields where an item is supposed to be are colored in blue!

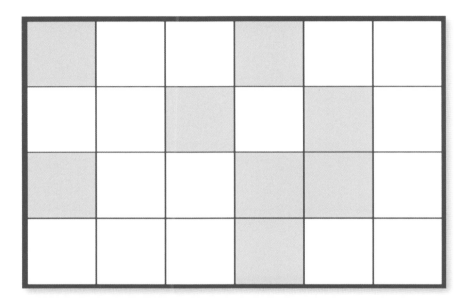

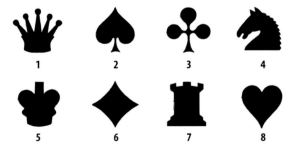

No Pain, No _____

Complete the following songs with the missing word.

1. Blowin' in the _____

2. November _____

3. Subterranean Homesick _____

4. When Irish Eyes Are _____

5. Benny and the _____

6. Sophisticated _____

7. Islands in the _____

8. A Hard Day's _____

9. Purple _____

10. Give It Up or Turn It _____

11. A-Tisket, A- _____

12. To Be Young, Gifted, and _____

13. Proud _____

14. I Can See for _____

15. Up Where We _____

No Pain, No _____

Complete the following movie titles with the missing word.

1. *Sophie's* _____

2. *The Safety of* _____

3. *Save the Last* _____

4. *I'm All Right* _____

5. *Lost in* _____

6. *Bad Day at Black* _____

7. *The Unbearable Lightness of* _____

8. *Unfaithfully* _____

9. *The Passion of the* _____

10. *Calendar* _____

11. *A Room with a* _____

12. *Dazed and* _____

13. *The Neverending* _____

14. *The Calcium* _____

15. *Ghost Dog: The Way of the* _____

Working the Memory Muscle

Take a minute to memorize the eight words below without looking at the bottom half of the page.

automobile

boat

information

bear

jam

parasol

marriage

cocoa

Now cover up the list of words and answer the following questions:

1. Which word in the list has no plural form?

_____

2. How many abstract words are there in the list? What are they?

_____

3. Which words in the list can be both a noun and a verb?

_____

4. Which words on the list are edible?

_____

Working the Memory Muscle

Take a minute to memorize the eight words below without looking at the bottom half of the page.

jersey

brown

apple pie

spinach

particularity

vanity

purple

hurry

Now cover up the list of words and answer the following questions:

1. Are any colors in the list? If so, which?

_____

2. Are there any fruit names in the list? If so, which?

_____

3. What, if any, abstract words are on the list?

_____

4. Which word is also the name of a state?

_____

The Final Rep

Carefully read the following five sentences and memorize the last word of each one. Then turn the page and continue.

After she had taken a shower, Christina started to get ready and put on her makeup.

The young man left the hospital and decided to go straight home to unpack.

Christian had ended up in a maze and struggled to keep his orientation.

A frog jumped across the puddle and tried to catch a passing butterfly.

As if they had planned it, they met right on time at the bottom of the stairs.

The Final Rep

According to what you have just read, can you answer this question?

A. Where was Christian?

- In a library
- In a forest
- In a maze

B. Can you now write down the last word of each sentence?

Sentence 1: _____

Sentence 2: _____

Sentence 3: _____

Sentence 4: _____

Sentence 5: _____

The Final Rep

Carefully read the following five sentences and memorize the last word of each one. Then turn the page and continue.

The museum doors closed and finally the building became quiet.

After the lawn had been mown Wendy went inside for a cold drink.

The mailman rang the bell and waited for Mrs. Salenger to open the door and take the parcel.

As she was lying on the lawn Jenny thought that the deep blue sky really was beautiful.

At the junction Sam and Matt couldn't decide which way to go and decided to take the road toward the east.

The Final Rep

According to what you have just read, can you answer this question?

A. Which kind of building becomes quiet?

- A hospital
- A bus station
- A museum

B. Can you now write down the last word of each sentence?

Sentence 1: _____

Sentence 2: _____

Sentence 3: _____

Sentence 4: _____

Sentence 5: _____

Opposing Muscle Groups

A. Find the opposite words for the 10 following words. The first letter has been given as a clue.

1. hypotension: h_____   **6.** compulsory: o_____

2. confess: d_____   **7.** objectivity: s_____

3. generous: s_____   **8.** authorized: u_____

4. nocturnal: d_____   **9.** sterile: f_____

5. convex: c_____   **10.** unique: c_____

B. Which are the two synonyms in each word series?

1. mood   habit   behavior   attitude   pose

2. suspicious   confident   fishy   quiet   obvious

3. eligible   intelligible   intelligent   understandable   understanding

4. chaperone   nanny   laundress   governess   nun

5. safety   honesty   probity   caution   cleanliness

Opposing Muscle Groups

A. Find the opposite words for the 10 following words. The first letter has been given as a clue.

1. flawless: i_____   **6.** bizarre: n_____

2. alone: t_____   **7.** flexible: r_____

3. enormous: t_____   **8.** extraordinary: m_____

4. synonym: a_____   **9.** important: t_____

5. partly: w_____   **10.** natural: a_____

B. Which are the two synonyms in each word series?

1. great   genuine   true   serious   sincere

2. uncommon   whiny   weird   eerie   custom

3. perusal   creation   inspired   colorful   inspection

4. restrained   limited   strained   closed   lifted

5. war   turnip   riot   fight   turmoil

Muscle Groups

Sort all the words in the list below into four categories and then give each category a title.

snorkel	club	fins	discus	driver
hammer	tank	hunting crop	iron	javelin
pole	putter	boat	reins	mask
saddle	shot	spurs	stirrup	tee

_____
TITLE

_____
TITLE

_____
TITLE

_____
TITLE

Muscle Groups

Sort all the words in the list below into four categories and then give each category a title.

Amun	Anubis	Aphrodite	Athena	Bacchus
Brahma	Diana	Dyonisus	Eros	Ganesh
Hathor	Horus	Isis	Juno	Kali
Mars	Neptune	Poseidon	Shiva	Vishnu

TITLE	TITLE	TITLE	TITLE

The Incomplete Workout

Look at the picture below. One tile is missing. Select the missing piece.

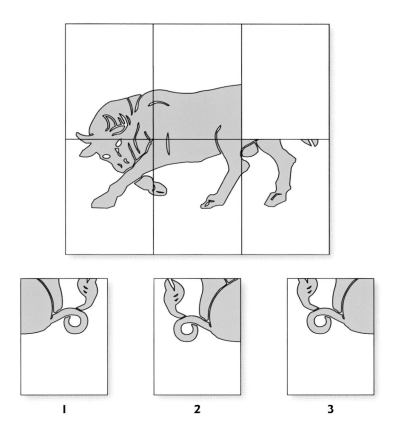

The Incomplete Workout

Look at the picture below. One tile is missing. Select the missing piece.

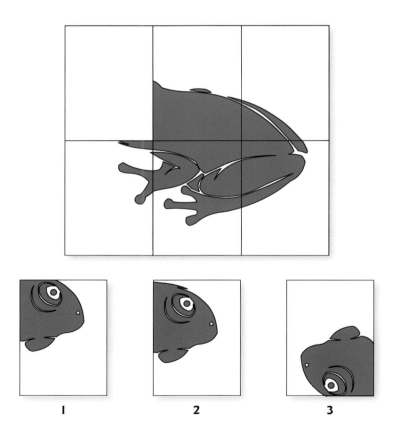

1   2   3

The Answers Are in the Stars

Of the nine words in each list below, only six can be placed in the star. Arrows indicate the direction in which each word is placed. To assist you, one letter has already been placed in each star. Try to fill in the two stars in five minutes or less.

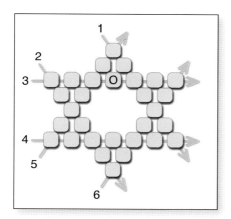
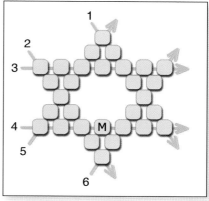

SERPENT	CELSIUS
TRIPLET	CORDAGE
TACKLES	GOLDEYE
CALORIE	MEASURE
GOLDEYE	MEETING
CYCLING	PILGRIM
PUMPKIN	PRIMATE
SCHOLAR	STATURE
SLIPPER	TERMITE

The Answers Are in the Stars

Of the nine words in each list below, only six can be placed in the star. Arrows indicate the direction in which each word is placed. To assist you, one letter has already been placed in each star. Try to fill in the two stars in five minutes or less.

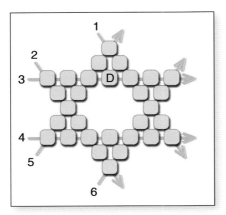
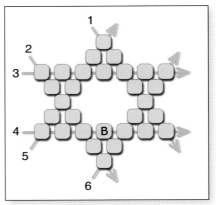

BANDAGE	APPOINT
BIVOUAC	CONCORD
CADETTE	CORONER
CUSTARD	DELIGHT
PUDDING	DOUBTER
SANDLOT	GENERAL
SAVINGS	GLOBULE
SHUDDER	LUNETTE
STARTER	PROBATE

Muscle Memory

Carefully look at the following composition. Then turn the page and continue the exercise.

Muscle Memory

Can you answer the following questions?

1. How many different hat shapes are there?

_____

2. What color are the masks?

_____

3. Are all crowns the same color?

_____

4. Can you partially see the inside of the crowns?

_____

Muscle Memory

Carefully look at the following composition. Then turn the page and continue the exercise.

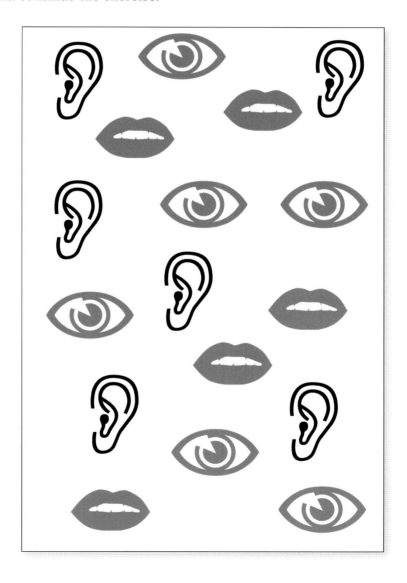

Muscle Memory

Can you answer the following questions?

1. Are the lips male or female?

_____

2. Do the eyes have lashes?

_____

3. Are the lips closed or half-closed?

_____

4. Are the ears you saw left or right ears?

_____

Pencils Up!

Link the 12 sunflowers on this page without raising your pencil. You cannot touch the other flowers, and you cannot go between two flowers more than once!

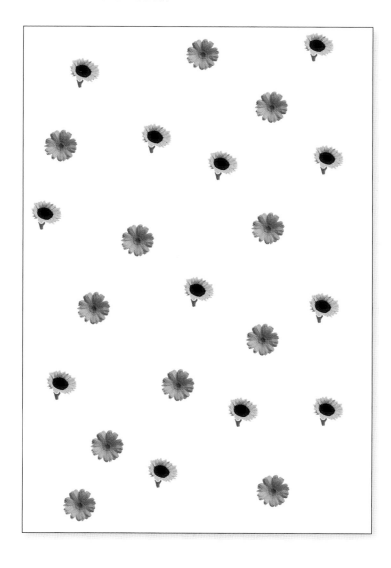

Pencils Up!

Link the 10 green oak leaves on this page without raising your pencil. You cannot touch the other leaves, and you cannot go between two leaves more than once!

Hard Exercises

Warm-Ups

Do you know the answers to these common-knowledge questions? Shake up your brain and find out.

1. In Greek mythology, who did Ariadne give her famous red thread to?

    a. Jason   **b.** Theseus   **c.** Odysseus

2. Which color cannot be found on the Romanian flag?

    a. green   **b.** red   **c.** blue

3. Which Italian composer wrote the opera *Aïda*?

    a. Vivaldi   **b.** Verdi   **c.** Rossini

4. How many players are there on a soccer team?

    a. 9   **b.** 10   **c.** 11

5. Conakry is the capital of which African country?

    a. Togo   **b.** Benin   **c.** Guinea

6. Which unit of pressure is the equivalent of one newton per square meter?

    a. pascal   **b.** torr   **c.** bar

7. Which degenerative disorder of the central nervous system often impairs motor skills, speech, and other functions?

    a. diabetes   **b.** osteoporosis   **c.** Parkinson's disease

8. What is the smallest planet of the solar system?

    a. Venus   **b.** Uranus   **c.** Earth

Warm-Ups

Do you know the answers to these common-knowledge questions? Shake up your brain and find out.

1. What is the first name of the French painter Cézanne?
   a. Henri   **b.** Paul   **c.** Pierre

2. Which country is Greenland closest to?
   a. Iceland   **b.** Canada   **c.** Finland

3. Which was the maiden name of the physicist and chemist Marie Curie?
   a. Belova   **b.** Sklodowska   **c.** Krakowsky

4. Which one of these Charlie Chaplin films was a sound film?
   a. *City Lights*   **b.** *The Kid*   **c.** *Monsieur Verdoux*

5. Apart from Chile, which other South American country does not share a border with Brazil?
   a. Ecuador   **b.** Colombia   **c.** Peru

6. What is the capital city of Eritrea?
   a. Malabo   **b.** Banjul   **c.** Asmara

7. Which famous French writer wrote the novel *Thérèse Raquin*?
   a. Emile Zola   **b.** Victor Hugo   **c.** Georges Sand

8. What is the name of the famous train that runs between Paris and Istanbul?
   a. Rheingold Express   **b.** Orient Express
   c. Trans-Siberian Railway

Daily Workout

Can you remember in which year these historical events occurred?

1. The Battle of Gettysburg

_____

2. The beginning of the Cold War

_____

3. The assassination of President John F. Kennedy

_____

4. The establishment of the Dutch East India Company

_____

5. The Great Fire of London

_____

6. The first report of AIDS

_____

7. The death of Genghis Khan

_____

8. The British declaration of war on Japan

_____

Daily Workout

Can you remember in which year these historical events occurred?

1. The end of Prohibition in the United States

---

2. The Smoot-Hawley Tariff Act

---

3. The invasion of Normandy

---

4. The Treaty of Antwerp

---

5. The Battles of Saratoga

---

6. The invention of movable type printing

---

7. The first Harley-Davidson ever sold

---

8. The start of the construction of the White House

Interval Training

Can you put back together the 20 multisyllabic words that have been split and spread across the grid? Watch out, each syllable can be used only once, and the splits may not necessarily be the syllable splits you find in the dictionary!

TIP: *All words belong to the category "Agriculture."*

pes	ter	try	re	dry	side	to	kohl
king	bree	ce	try	hay	re	mil	poul
pro	per	mill	wi	barb	tion	ban	tor
or	cide	ti	ta	ce	trac	son	har
rer	pea	ga	cken	ter	al	ta	her
far	hus	ding	la	wind	bi	ming	ves
ra	stack	bo	coun	nic	ding	po	sant
chi	ra	plan	ry	ty	cing	sea	le

Your answers:

1. _____   11. _____

2. _____   12. _____

3. _____   13. _____

4. _____   14. _____

5. _____   15. _____

6. _____   16. _____

7. _____   17. _____

8. _____   18. _____

9. _____   19. _____

10. _____   20. _____

Interval Training

Can you put back together the 20 multisyllabic words that have been split and spread across the grid? Watch out, each syllable can be used only once, and the splits may not necessarily be the syllable splits you find in the dictionary!

TIP: *All words belong to the category "Business."*

in	quo	as	au	com	part	der	per
de	rupt	ca	ma	ger	turn	son	pro
di	o	sets	vent	ment	op	tor	chair
ver	pa	hol	set	take	ger	tle	na
bar	tion	ma	sol	va	trans	ban	ger
ment	led	nage	di	share	gain	ta	lue
ny	rec	ker	man	ment	bank	tion	mer
fer	ver	tal	nel	fit	o	tor	pi

Your answers:

1. _____   11. _____

2. _____   12. _____

3. _____   13. _____

4. _____   14. _____

5. _____   15. _____

6. _____   16. _____

7. _____   17. _____

8. _____   18. _____

9. _____   19. _____

10. _____   20. _____

Lateral Rows

For each row, circle which of the three words is spelled correctly.

1.	wroght	wrawght	wrought
2.	gynecologist	gynecolojist	gynecollogist
3.	wharf	whorf	warf
4.	picolo	piccolo	picollo
5.	azimut	azimuth	azzimuth
6.	nuclear	newclear	nucleer
7.	lyrissism	lyricysm	lyricism
8.	gaselle	gazelle	gazell
9.	nuisance	nuisence	newsance
10.	makadam	maccadam	macadam
11.	gnocci	gnocchi	gnocchy
12.	opalescant	opelescent	opalescent
13.	piaza	piazza	piadsa
14.	jitny	jittney	jitney
15.	azurit	azuritt	azurite
16.	gecko	gecco	geccho

Lateral Rows

For each row, circle which of the three words is spelled correctly.

1. newance | nuance | nuence
2. nullification | nullyfication | nulification
3. macaroon | maccaroon | maccarroon
4. haylo | halo | heylo
5. jonquile | jonquill | jonquil
6. aygis | aegys | aegis
7. afar | affar | effar
8. dialysis | dyalisis | dialisys
9. fucsia | fuchsia | fuccsia
10. fiascco | fiascho | fiasco
11. lumbaggo | lumbaego | lumbago
12. vorassity | voracity | vorasity
13. robest | robust | robbust
14. satchel | satshell | sacchel
15. Gernsey | Gernzy | Guernsey
16. tonsilitis | tonsillitis | tonsylitis

Bio-Feedback

Whose life is described below?

I was a French chemist and microbiologist born on December 27, 1922, in Dole, the Jura region of France where I later had my house and laboratory. My excellent school results led my college headmaster to advise me to apply to the Ecole Normale Supérieure. After that, I briefly taught physics at Dijon Lycée in 1848 and then moved on to being a chemistry professor at Strasburg College where I met Marie Laurent, whom I married in May 1849 and had five children with.

I am famous for my remarkable breakthroughs in the causes and prevention of disease. I managed to reduce mortality from childbed fever and produced the first vaccine for rabies. I am most famous for my procedure to stop milk and wine from causing sickness. That procedure is named after me. Together with Ferdinand Cohn and Robert Koch, I am considered one of the three founders of microbiology. Today, a French nonprofit private foundation for the study of biology, microorganisms, diseases, and vaccines I once founded is still named after me and is one of the world's leading research centers.

Bio-Feedback

Whose life is described below?

I was born in St. Louis, Missouri, on June 3, 1906, and I started my career as a celebrated dancer but later became more famous for my voice. One of my nicknames was the "Créole Goddess," and I was the first African-American woman to be featured in major movies and to become a world-famous entertainer.

At the age of 12 I left school and soon started dancing and performing on the street. I entered vaudeville at age 15, moved on to New York City during the Harlem Renaissance, and performed in the chorus of most popular Broadway revues. Back then, I was billed as the "highest-paid chorus girl in vaudeville."

In October 1925, I performed in Paris, France, at the Théatre des Champs-Elysées, and my erotic dancing—not to mention being nearly nude on stage—made me an instant success. After a successful European tour, I settled in France and eventually became a citizen. When the Nazis occupied France during World War II, I was such a popular personality that the Nazis did not dare harm me, so I had the opportunity to work underground for the Resistance, passing on information coded in my sheet music. In the 1950s I also supported the American Civil Rights movements from France.

While my professional life was incredibly successful, my personal life was less so. I went through six marriages, not all of them being legal. I died on April 12, 1975, at the age of 68 after a cerebral hemorrhage.

The Proper Form

Pay attention to the shape and position of the 10 icons in the grid. Then turn the page and continue the exercise.

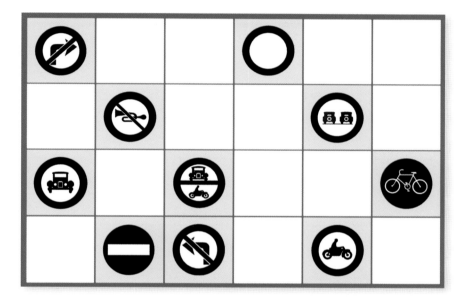

The Proper Form

Can you place all 10 elements correctly back into the grid?

TIP: *The fields where an item is supposed to be are colored in blue!*

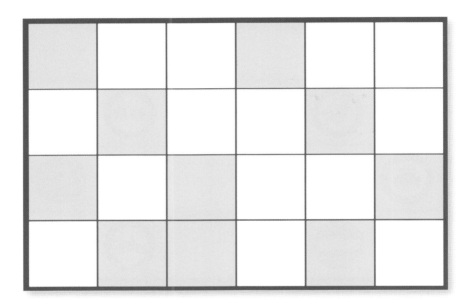

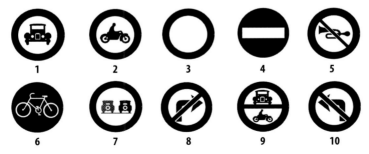

The Proper Form

Pay attention to the shape and position of the 10 icons in the grid. Then turn the page and continue the exercise.

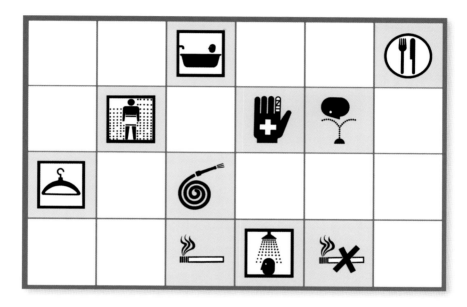

The Proper Form

Can you place all 10 elements correctly back into the grid?

TIP: *The fields where an item is supposed to be are colored in blue!*

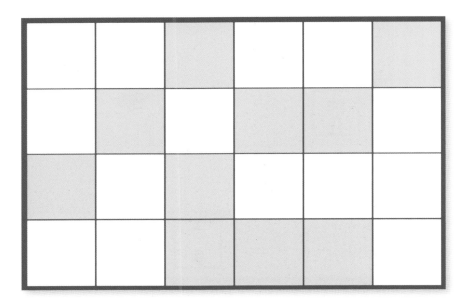

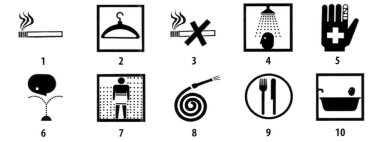

No Pain, No _____

Complete the following chemical compounds with the missing word.

1. Carbon _____
2. Boric _____
3. Lithium aluminium _____
4. Cacodylic _____
5. Radon _____
6. Baking _____
7. Folic _____
8. Arsenic _____
9. Mesityl _____
10. Acetic _____
11. Allyl _____
12. Furfuryl _____
13. Malachite _____
14. Petroleum _____
15. Nile _____

No Pain, No _____

Complete the following novel titles with the missing word.

1. *The Last of the* _____

2. *Lord of the* _____

3. *A Farewell to* _____

4. *Sunday After the* _____

5. *Invisible* _____

6. *To Kill a* _____

7. *Smiley's* _____

8. *On Wings of* _____

9. *The Celestine* _____

10. *Little Lord* _____

11. *The Brothers* _____

12. *Framley* _____

13. *Great* _____

14. *Jonathan Livingston* _____

15. *The Stone* _____

Working the Memory Muscle

Take a minute to memorize the 10 words below without looking at the bottom half of the page.

nullification	**chacha**
sure-fire	**dockage**
publicity	**tutu**
gardening	**hoover**
step	**bathroom**

Now cover up the list of words and answer the following questions:

1. Which of the words are related to the theme "Dance"?

_____

2. Which, if any, words on the list are compound words?

_____

3. Which of the words comes first alphabetically?

_____

4. Which word has the most letters?

_____

5. Which, if any, of the words are related to the theme "Home"?

_____

Working the Memory Muscle

Take a minute to memorize the 10 words below without looking at the bottom half of the page.

negligee	**tutelary**
babysitter	**aficionado**
dolce vita	**turtleneck**
baccarat	**wit**
poaching	**liaison**

Now cover up the list of words and answer the following questions:

1. How many foreign words are there on the list? Which are they?

_____

2. What are the two shortest words?

_____

3. Are there any names of games? If so, which ones?

_____

4. Which words have in some way to do with animals?

_____

5. Do you remember any abstract words? Which?

_____

The Final Rep

Carefully read the following six sentences and memorize the last word of each one. Then turn the page and continue.

The peasants were powerless against the locust invasion that destroyed their crops.

Audrey makes such good cherry pies that they always get eaten up.

June agreed to watch the neighbors' cat while they were on holidays.

The church members organized a raffle for a charity event.

When James fell down he dragged a dish of asparagus with him.

The singer left the press conference without any further explanations.

The Final Rep

According to what you have just read, can you answer this question?

A. What did June do for her neighbors?

- Watch the cat
- Water the plants
- Watch the apartment

B. Can you now write down the last word of each sentence?

Sentence 1: _____

Sentence 2: _____

Sentence 3: _____

Sentence 4: _____

Sentence 5: _____

Sentence 6: _____

The Final Rep

Carefully read the following six sentences and memorize the last word of each one. Then turn the page and continue.

Given the fierceness of the woman, Joan thought it was better to give up and go home.

Allan had been badly beaten up in a back alley and had to be sent to the hospital.

As she had chosen to wear a red dress, Wanda couldn't decide which shoes to wear.

Mr. and Mrs. Absalom came home from the gala right after the burglars had left.

John found the manor empty and went to see where his friends had gone.

The aria chosen by the diva was a huge success with the audience.

The Final Rep

According to what you have just read, can you answer this question?

A. Where did Allan get beaten up?

- In the woods
- In a back alley
- In a bar

B. Can you now write down the last word of each sentence?

Sentence 1: _____

Sentence 2: _____

Sentence 3: _____

Sentence 4: _____

Sentence 5: _____

Sentence 6: _____

Opposing Muscle Groups

A. Find the opposite words for the 10 following words. The first letter has been given as a clue.

1. philanthropist: m_____

6. painful: p_____

2. virtual: r_____

7. hypertrophy: a_____

3. monotheism: p_____

8. absolute: r_____

4. anglophobe: a_____

9. enslave: f_____

5. host: g_____

10. dwarfism: g_____

B. Which are the two synonyms in each word series?

1. malaria   icterus   tuberculosis   jaundice   pox

2. kiwi   ibis   apteryx   flamingo   stork

3. pathetic   plebeian   rustic   urban   piteous

4. pallid   variable   talkative   quirky   versatile

5. grinder   sieve   mill   funnel   winder

Opposing Muscle Groups

A. Find the opposite words for the 10 following words. The first letter has been given as a clue.

1. anisogamy: i_____   **6.** melting: f_____

2. measurable: i_____   **7.** ubiquitous: a_____

3. allegro: l_____   **8.** abductor: a_____

4. pulchritude: u_____   **9.** order: c_____

5. monaural: s_____   **10.** centripetal: c_____

B. Which are the two synonyms in each word series?

1. Minoan   Egyptian   Hellenic   Roman   Greek

2. hector   fight   mercenary   bully   hectare

3. horizontal   orthogonal   perpendicular parallel   tangent

4. unisexed   intersexed   homogeneous androgen   hermaphrodite

5. mean   demeanor   diminish   mien   way

Muscle Groups

Sort all the words in the list below into four categories and then give each category a title.

atmosphere	bar	barrel	barye	bushel
carat	fathom	gallon	inch	meter
mile	ounce	pascal	pint	pound
stere	talent	ton	torr	yard

| TITLE | TITLE | TITLE | TITLE |

Muscle Groups

Sort all the words in the list below into four categories and then give each category a title.

anaconda	asp	ateles	bonobo	cobra
crotalinae	fruit bat	gazelle	gemsbock	gibbon
gorilla	impala	mamba	mandrill	nyctalus
oryx	pipistrellus	plecotus	springbok	vampire

TITLE	TITLE	TITLE	TITLE

The Incomplete Workout

Look at the picture below. One tile is missing. Select the missing piece.

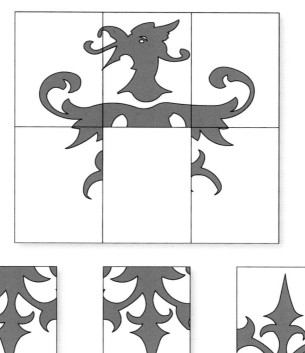

1

2

3

The Incomplete Workout

Look at the picture below. One tile is missing. Select the missing piece.

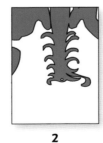

1   2   3

The Answers Are in the Stars

Of the nine words in each list below, only six can be placed in the star. Arrows indicate the direction in which each word is placed. Try to fill in the two stars in five minutes or less.

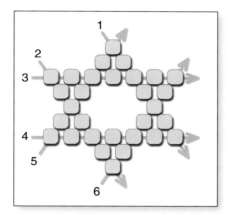
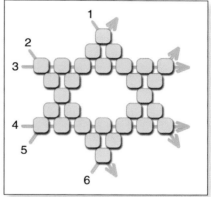

AMATEUR	ABUSAGE
ATTACHE	ALIMENT
BALANCE	ARSENIC
INGENUE	AVARICE
RECLUSE	CORTEGE
REFUGEE	FERRULE
RUPTURE	MASCARA
STARTER	MINARET
STEEPLE	PIRANHA

The Answers Are in the Stars

Of the nine words in each list below, only six can be placed in the star. Arrows indicate the direction in which each word is placed. Try to fill in the two stars in five minutes or less.

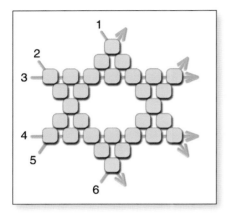 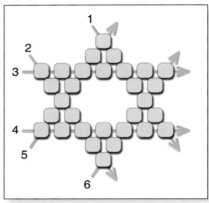

BARGAIN	EPSILON
BLOUSON	MAGNATE
NATURAL	MENTHOL
NEUTRON	PERIGEE
NOSTRIL	POULTRY
NULLITY	PRELUDE
PROGRAM	PROCESS
SEAGULL	PROGRAM
SIRLOIN	SAUSAGE

Muscle Memory

Carefully look at the following composition. Then turn the page and continue the exercise.

Muscle Memory

Can you answer the following questions?

1. How many different cloud shapes are there?

_____

2. What color are the suns?

_____

3. How many pink snowflakes are there?

_____

4. Is rain falling from certain clouds?

_____

5. Are all clouds the same color?

_____

Muscle Memory

Carefully look at the following composition. Then turn the page and continue the exercise.

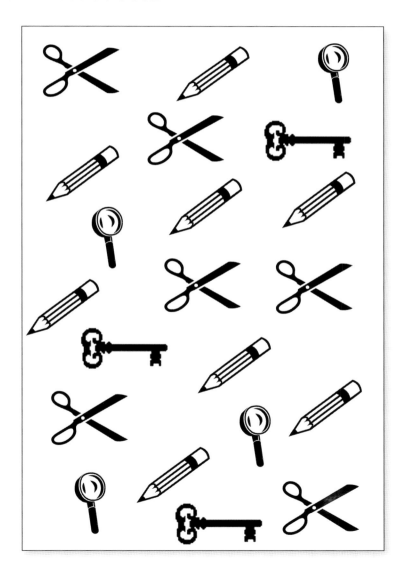

Muscle Memory

Can you answer the following questions?

1. How many different types of elements are there?

_____

2. Are the scissors open or closed?

_____

3. Which side does the pencil lead point to?

_____

4. How many keys are in the image?

_____

5. Which elements could be used in an office?

_____

Pencils Up!

Link the 12 red roses on this page without raising your pencil. You cannot touch the other red flowers, and you cannot go between two flowers more than once!

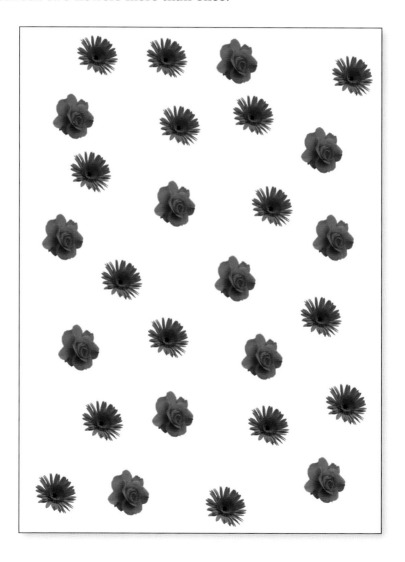

Pencils Up!

Link the 12 maple leaves on this page without raising your pencil. You cannot touch the other leaves, and you cannot go between two leaves more than once!

Can You Beat Hercules?

Link the seven green oak leaves and the seven raspberries alternately on this page without raising your pencil. You cannot touch the other leaves and fruits, you cannot link two leaves, and you cannot use a leaf or raspberry twice!

Solutions

Easy Exercises

Warm-Ups
1. c: Edgar Allan Poe
2. b: caravel
3. c: basketball
4. c: rat snake
5. a: Italy
6. c: Watson
7. c: green
8. a: The approval of the Declaration of Independence

Warm-Ups
1. a: spider
2. a: Matt Groening
3. c: Popeye the Sailor
4. b: 18th
5. b: Little Bighorn
6. a: Finland
7. c: dog
8. b: Steven Spielberg

Daily Workout
1. 1969
2. 1912
3. 1773
4. 1929
5. 1492
6. 1975
7. 1989
8. 1776

Daily Workout
1. 1939
2. 1876
3. 1986
4. 1997
5. 1984
6. 1981
7. 1953
8. 1616

Interval Training
1. beetroot
2. breadfruit
3. carrot
4. pickle
5. durban
6. kiwi
7. kumquat
8. lemon
9. lychee
10. mango
11. melon
12. lettuce
13. parsley
14. parsnip
15. pepper
16. pumpkin
17. onion
18. rhubarb
19. spinach
20. sweetcorn

Interval Training
1. Athens
2. Bahrain
3. Beijing
4. Berlin
5. Cairo
6. Dublin
7. Hanoi

8. Lima
9. London
10. Madrid
11. Moscow
12. Nassau
13. Oslo
14. Paris
15. Tallin
16. Quito
17. Sydney
18. Tehran
19. Warsaw
20. Zurich

Lateral Rows
1. insolvency
2. valuable
3. accordance
4. occurrence
5. insourcing
6. literature
7. oceanology
8. management
9. yogurt
10. trainee
11. occupancy
12. hazard
13. occlusive
14. integrate
15. youngster
16. azure

Lateral Rows
1. vitamin
2. babywear
3. dabbler
4. tobacco
5. weekend
6. wealth
7. fruitful
8. jockey

9. ability
10. beach
11. ozone
12. hiccup
13. genealogy
14. varsity
15. junior
16. doctor

Bio-Feedback
Frieda Kahlo

Bio-Feedback
Mikhail Gorbachev

No Pain, No _____
1. room
2. promise
3. cake
4. life
5. duckling
6. ropes
7. circle
8. hoops
9. cucumber
10. boat
11. case
12. goods
13. turn
14. hat
15. murder

No Pain, No _____
1. cookies
2. carne
3. beef
4. pie
5. cookies
6. puppies
7. cocktail
8. sundae

9. rings
10. butter
11. cake
12. potatoes
13. cob
14. cheese
15. cake

Working the Memory Muscle
1. The animals in the list are **elephant**, **cow**, and **shrimp**.
2. The abstract words are **design** and **part**.
3. **Cow** is the shortest word in the list.

Working the Memory Muscle
1. **Tea** is the drink in the list.
2. The profession named in the list is **chef**.
3. A **feather** can be found on a bird.

The Final Rep
A. Roast lamb
B. cousin, potatoes, house, days

The Final Rep
A. Thunderstorm
B. lawn, yard, resort, city

Opposing Muscle Groups
A.
1. fat
2. beautiful
3. mean
4. clean
5. weak
6. low
7. false

8. dry
9. careless
10. narrow

B.
1. mom/mother
2. door/gate
3. issue/problem
4. look/appearance
5. nausea/queasiness

Opposing Muscle Groups
A.
1. dishonest
2. small
3. hard
4. cowardly
5. bad
6. thin
7. open
8. seldom
9. old
10. senior

B.
1. flawless/perfect
2. sadness/grief
3. magic/witchcraft
4. bottle/flagon
5. missive/letter

Muscle Groups
Types of cheese
brie
cheddar
gorgonzola
gouda
mozzarella

Types of cake
sponge
cupcake
pound
fruit
tiramisu

Types of cold meat
bologna
liverwurst
ham
prosciutto
salami

Types of hot meat dishes
hot dog
leg of lamb
roast beef
spare ribs
steak

Muscle Groups
Types of garden plants
acacia
geranium
laurel
moss
nettle

Types of fruit
apricot
blueberry
cherry
date
pineapple

Types of salad
chicory
endive
escarole

lettuce
rocket

Types of cereal
corn
oat
rice
rye
wheat

The Incomplete Workout
The missing tile is number 1.

The Incomplete Workout
The missing tile is number 2.

The Answers Are in the Stars
First Star
1. diploma
2. eclipse
3. example
4. paprika
5. pollard
6. episode

Second Star
1. granite
2. plastic
3. primary
4. methane
5. meaning
6. charity

The Answers Are in the Stars
First Star
1. lottery
2. caption
3. curette
4. avidity
5. apparel
6. naivete

Second Star
1. soilage
2. parsnip
3. premise
4. panache
5. parsecs
6. package

Muscle Memory
1. There are nine frogs.
2. The rats heads are turned to the left.
3. The third animal is a duck.

Muscle Memory
1. There are 21 elements in total.
2. The straws are turned toward the right side of the glass.
3. There are eight salt shakers.

Medium Exercises

Warm-Ups
1. b: Jupiter
2. c: 24
3. b: March 17
4. a: Cu
5. c: Mark Twain
6. b: platypus
7. c: Switzerland
8. c: Southampton

Warm-Ups
1. c: Agra
2. b: Olive Oyl
3. c: Dirham
4. c: 11
5. a: War
6. c: Alaska
7. a: John Lennon
8. b: Pulitzer Prize

Daily Workout
1. 1991
2. 1945
3. 1815
4. 1945
5. 1981
6. 1865
7. 1993
8. 1870

Daily Workout
1. 1895
2. 1886
3. 1889
4. 1861

5. 1957
6. 1789
7. 1835
8. 44 BC

Interval Training
1. acacia
2. baobab
3. butternut
4. catalpa
5. cedar
6. douglas-fir
7. hemlock
8. hornbeam
9. juniper
10. ligustrum
11. linden
12. magnolia
13. maple
14. mimosa
15. red cedar
16. sassafras
17. sequoia
18. sycamore
19. tuliptree
20. willow

Interval Training
1. apartment
2. chesterfield
3. cabinet
4. candle
5. casserole
6. chamberpot
7. countertop

8. credenza
9. cupboard
10. folding screen
11. furnishing
12. futon
13. living room
14. painting
15. parasol
16. photograph
17. recliner
18. sideboard
19. sofa
20. waterbed

Lateral Rows
1. kosher
2. docent
3. moose
4. numb
5. hedonism
6. cluster
7. macabre
8. bizarre
9. brew
10. humble
11. backboard
12. vertical
13. goblet
14. amazing
15. gobsmacked
16. tiara

Lateral Rows
1. bobsleigh
2. docility
3. biblical
4. amused
5. muesli
6. nugget
7. clue
8. macaroni

9. thyme
10. woeful
11. onwards
12. mucous
13. boiled
14. mudguard
15. jubilee
16. kernel

Bio-Feedback
Daniel Day-Lewis

Bio-Feedback
Steven Patrick Morrissey from The Smiths

No Pain, No _____
1. Wind
2. Rain
3. Blues
4. Smiling
5. Jets
6. Lady
7. Stream
8. Night
9. Rain
10. Loose
11. Tasket
12. Black
13. Mary
14. Miles
15. Belong

No Pain, No _____
1. Choice
2. Objects
3. Dance
4. Jack
5. Translation
6. Rock
7. Being

8. Yours
9. Christ
10. Girls
11. View
12. Confused
13. Story
14. Kid
15. Samurai

Working the Memory Muscle
1. **Information** is the word that cannot be used in the plural.
2. There are two abstract words: **marriage** and **information**.
3. **Bear**, **boat**, and **jam** can be both a noun and a verb.
4. **Jam** and **cocoa** are edible.

Working the Memory Muscle
1. The colors **purple** and **brown** are in the list.
2. There are **no fruits** in the list.
3. The abstract words are **brown**, **particularity**, **vanity**, **purple**, and **hurry**.
4. **Jersey** is the name of a state.

The Final Rep
A. In a maze
B. makeup, unpack, orientation, butterfly, stairs

The Final Rep
A. A museum
B. quiet, drink, parcel, beautiful, east

Opposing Muscle Groups
A.
1. hypertension
2. deny
3. stingy
4. diurnal
5. concave
6. optional
7. subjectivity
8. unofficial
9. fertile
10. common

B.
1. behavior/attitude
2. suspicious/fishy
3. intelligible/understandable
4. nanny/governess
5. honesty/probity

Opposing Muscle Groups
A.
1. imperfect
2. together
3. tiny
4. antonym
5. wholly
6. normal
7. rigid
8. mediocre
9. trivial
10. artificial

B.
1. genuine/sincere
2. weird/eerie
3. perusal/inspection
4. restrained/limited
5. riot/turmoil

Muscle Groups
Scuba equipment
snorkel
fins
tank
mask
boat

Golfing equipment
club
driver
iron
putter
tee

Athletics equipment
discus
hammer
javelin
pole
shot

Horse riding equipment
hunting crop
reins
saddle
spurs
stirrup

Muscle Groups
Egyptian deities
Amun
Anubis
Hathor
Horus
Isis

Greek deities
Aphrodite
Athena
Dyonysus
Eros
Poseidon

Roman deities
Bacchus
Diane
Juno
Mars
Neptune

Hindu deities
Brahma
Ganesh
Kali
Shiva
Vishnu

The Incomplete Workout
The missing tile is number 3.

The Incomplete Workout
The missing tile is number 1.

The Answers Are in the Stars
First Star
1. serpent
2. cycling
3. calorie
4. triplet
5. tackles
6. goldeye

Second Star
1. measure
2. celsius
3. cordage
4. primate
5. pilgrim
6. stature

The Answers Are in the Stars

First Star
1. starter
2. bivouac
3. bandage
4. shudder
5. savings
6. cadette

Second Star
1. lunette
2. concord
3. coroner
4. globule
5. general
6. doubter

Muscle Memory

1. There are two different hat shapes.
2. The masks are black.
3. No, the crowns are either pink or black.
4. Yes, you can partially see the inside of the crowns.

Muscle Memory

1. The lips are female.
2. No, there aren't any lashes.
3. The lips are half-closed.
4. The ears are left ears.

Hard Exercises

Warm-Ups
1. b: Theseus
2. a: green
3. b: Verdi
4. c: 11
5. c: Guinea
6. a: pascal
7. c: Parkinson's disease
8. a: Venus

Warm-Ups
1. b: Paul
2. b: Canada
3. b: Sklodowska
4. c: *Monsieur Verdoux*
5. a: Ecuador
6. c: Asmara
7. a: Emile Zola
8. b: Orient Express

Daily Workout
1. 1863
2. 1945
3. 1963
4. 1602
5. 1666
6. 1981
7. 1227
8. 1941

Daily Workout
1. 1933
2. 1930
3. 1944
4. 1609

5. 1777
6. 1439
7. 1904
8. 1792

Interval Training
1. barbwire
2. breeding
3. celery
4. cereal
5. chicken
6. countryside
7. farming
8. harvester
9. haystack
10. herding
11. husbandry
12. kohlrabi
13. laborer
14. milking
15. organic
16. peasant
17. pesticide
18. plantation
19. potato
20. poultry
21. property
22. season
23. terracing
24. tractor
25. windmill

Interval Training
1. assets
2. auditor

3. banker
4. bankrupt
5. bargain
6. capital
7. chairman
8. company
9. department
10. director
11. insolvent
12. ledger
13. management
14. manager
15. merger
16. option
17. personnel
18. profit
19. quotation
20. settlement
21. shareholder
22. takeover
23. transfer
24. turnover
25. value

Lateral Rows

1. wrought
2. gynecologist
3. wharf
4. piccolo
5. azimuth
6. nuclear
7. lyricism
8. gazelle
9. nuisance
10. macadam
11. gnocchi
12. opalescent
13. piazza
14. jitney
15. azurite
16. gecko

Lateral Rows

1. nuance
2. nullification
3. macaroon
4. halo
5. jonquil
6. aegis
7. afar
8. dialysis
9. fuchsia
10. fiasco
11. lumbago
12. voracity
13. robust
14. satchel
15. Guernsey
16. tonsillitis

Bio-Feedback
Louis Pasteur

Bio-Feedback
Josephine Baker

No Pain, No _____

1. dioxide
2. acid
3. hybride
4. acid
5. difluoride
6. soda
7. acid
8. trioxide
9. oxide
10. acid
11. chloride
12. alcohol
13. green
14. ether
15. red

No Pain, No _____
1. Mohicans
2. Flies
3. Arms
4. War
5. Man
6. Mockingbird
7. People
8. Eagles
9. Prophecy
10. Fauntleroy
11. Karamazov
12. Parsonage
13. Expectations
14. Seagull
15. Diaries

Working the Memory Muscle
1. **Chacha, tutu,** and **step** are all words related to the theme "Dance."
2. **Sure-fire** is a compound word.
3. **Bathroom** comes first alphabetically in the list.
4. The word with the most letters is **nullification**.
5. **Gardening, hoover,** and **bathroom** are related to the theme "Home."

Working the Memory Muscle
1. There are four foreign words in the list: **negligee, aficionado, dolce vita, baccarat.**
2. The two shortest words are **wit** and **liaison.**
3. **Baccarat** is a game.
4. **Poaching** and **turtleneck** are both in some way animal-related.

5. The abstract words are **tutelary, aficionado, dolce vita, wit, poaching,** and **liaison.**

The Final Rep
A. Watch the cat
B. crops, up, holidays, event, him, explanations

The Final Rep
A. In a back alley
B. home, hospital, wear, left, gone, audience

Opposing Muscle Groups
A.
1. misanthrope
2. real
3. polytheism
4. anglophile
5. guest
6. painless
7. atrophy
8. relative
9. free
10. gigantism

B.
1. icterus/jaundice
2. kiwi/apteryx
3. pathetic/piteous
4. variable/versatile
5. grinder/mill

Opposing Muscle Groups
A.
1. isogamy
2. immeasurable
3. lento
4. ugliness

5. stereophonic
6. freezing
7. absent
8. adductor
9. chaos
10. centrifugal

B.
1. Hellenic/Greek
2. hector/bully
3. orthogonal/perpendicular
4. intersexed/hermaphrodite
5. demeanor/mien

Muscle Groups
Units of volume
barrel
bushel
gallon
pint
stere

Units of length
fathom
inch
meter
mile
yard

Units of mass
carat
ounce
pound
talent
ton

Units of pressure
atmosphere
bar

barye
pascal
torr

Muscle Groups
Snakes
anaconda
asp
cobra
crotalinae
mamba

Bats
fruit bat
nyctalus
pipistrellus
plecotus
vampire

Apes
ateles
bonobo
gibbon
gorilla
mandrill

Antelopes
gazelle
gemsbock
impala
oryx
springbok

The Incomplete Workout
The missing tile is number 2.

The Incomplete Workout
The missing tile is number 3.

The Answers Are in the Stars
First Star
1. recluse
2. amateur
3. attaché
4. steeple
5. starter
6. rupture

Second Star
1. cortège
2. mascara
3. minaret
4. avarice
5. arsenic
6. aliment

The Answers Are in the Stars
First Star
1. nostril
2. bargain
3. blouson
4. seagull
5. sirloin
6. neutron

Second Star
1. magnate
2. process
3. perigee
4. prelude
5. program
6. sausage

Muscle Memory
1. There are two different cloud shapes.
2. The suns are white.
3. There are six pink flakes.
4. Yes, rain is falling from certain clouds.
5. No, the clouds are either pink or black.

Muscle Memory
1. There are four different types of elements.
2. The scissors are open.
3. The pencil leads point to the left side.
4. There are three keys.
5. The scissors and the pencils could be used in an office.